ISBN (Paperback): 979-8-9884655-9-1
ISBN (eBook): 979-8-9884655-8-4

To my talented little piglets.

Mom

Thank you, Heavenly Father,
for helping me find my purpose.

Bella the little pig, her mom, and puppy Chocolate were on their way to school when they met someone new. Her mom said, "Hi! Who is this?"

Ms. Lauren Llama, the teacher, said, "This is my son, Mike; he will be in your class Bella."

The shy sheep did not speak and looked down.

BARN
SCHOOL

They meet Lisa, the cow; she asks,
"Do you want some apples?"

The sheep did not look up.

"He is new and will be in our class,"
Bella said.

The little sheep was quiet.

B
MATH
SCIENCE
HISTORY

At their desks, Troy the horse asked, "Who is that?"

"His name is Mike. Do you want an apple?" she asked.

"Neigh," said the horse.

"Are you sure? They're delicious," she said.

The sheep was busy looking at the mess around the pig's desk.

MIKE
BELLA
TROY

The others in the class wanted to know who the new student was.

Lisa, the cow, told William the wolf and Victoria, the ostrich, "He's very shy."

VICTORIA
William
LISA

Ms. Llama said, "Students, please welcome my son Mike to the class."

"Heyyy..." they all said.

M
MIKE
MATH
SCIENCE
HISTORY

On the way home, Bella asked Mike to walk with her.

They meet the wise old Goat.

"Do you want some apples?" asked the pig to the Goat.

"Naaah," he said, "Who is your new friend?"

"Baaah," said the sheep and then looked down.

When they got to her house, she said, "Let's play here."

The sheep looked around and saw all the trash and mess in the yard.

They went to Bella’s room, and she said, “We should have a welcome party for you.”

The sheep did not say anything and looked at her.

“What’s wrong?” asked Bella.

“We can’t have a party here; it’s a mess and needs a lot of cleaning,” said Mike.

LAUNDRY
CHIPS

That night Bella told her parents,
"Mom, Dad, I want to clean the house
and have a party."

Her dad said, "But, Bella, why clean?
We live in a pigsty. Do we have to?"

Her mom said, "Dear, that's a
wonderful idea!"

Both her parents said, "Oink."

Bella went to bed happy. That night she dreamed about inviting the others to her house and having a big party for the sheep.

LAUNDRY

The others talked about the shy sheep and the messy pig.

The horse asked, “Does he talk?”

“I don’t know,” said the ostrich.

The wolf said, “Maybe he doesn’t have a voice?”

“Oh, poor, poor sheep,” said the cow.

Bella and Mike meet the wise old Goat again. He asked, "Hayyyy...What's wrong?"

Bella said, "I want to have a party, and they won't come because my house is a mess."

"Well, why don't you help each other? Two is better than one, "said the Goat.

The sheep smiled.

They cleaned the pig's room, and the sheep started singing softly.

Mike said, "I like to sing when I clean; I wrote a song. Wanna hear it?"

"Oink!" said Bella.

He sang:
"If it's yucky and it's stinky."
"Baaah..."
"I will trashy. I will trashy."

LAUNDRY

Bella started to dance as she cleaned.

"If it's musty and it's dusty."
"Baaah..."
"I will wipey. I will wipey."

The sheep's voice got louder.

LAUNDRY
TRASH

Then they cleaned the rest of the house.

The shy sheep sang louder and louder.

"If I drop it. If I drop it."
"Baaah..."
"I will mop it. I will mop it."

The sheep and the pig danced and sang loudly.

TRASH
WASH

The pig had no idea that the sheep had a voice.

They were excited to have the party. Bella knew who would be singing that day.

At school, Ms. Llama invited all the students. She smiled and said, "Bella's family will have a party for Mike, and there will be a surprise."

P
PARTY
MATH
SCIENCE
HISTORY

At the party, the shy sheep got scared.

He said, "Maaaa…I can't do this.
I'm scaaarred."

Bella was ready; she said, "I thought that might happen. Here's something to help you."

It was a pair of dark sunglasses, so the sheep could not see when he sang.

The shy sheep wore the glasses, got on the stage, and started singing.

At first, it was soft, but then he got louder.

"BAAAHHH TO BE WILD," he sang loudly.

The others were surprised!

Mike, the shy sheep, had a loud, beautiful voice.

They listened and cheered.

"Sing Mike Sing," they shouted.

I hope you enjoyed the book and
that it encourages you to share love and
chase dreams.

For more inspirational books in the series,
visit: www.vatsanabooks.com.

www.ingramcontent.com/pod-product-compliance
Ingram Content Group UK Ltd.
Pitfield, Milton Keynes, MK11 3LW, UK
UKHW061950290726
14090UKWH00021B/1167

9 798988 465591